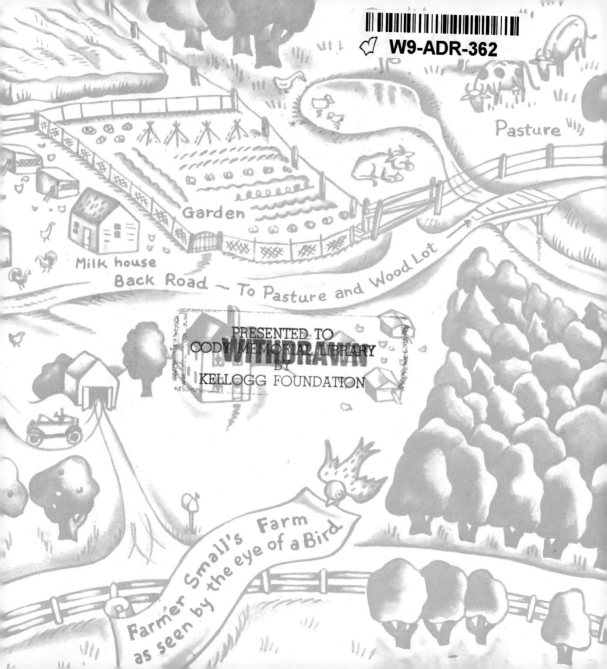

W9-ADR-362

Pasture

Garden

Milk house

Back Road ~ To Pasture and Wood Lot

Farmer Small's Farm
as seen by the eye of a Bird

The
LITTLE FARM

by LOIS LENSKI

HENRY Z. WALCK, INC.

For Nina and Toni

Library of Congress Catalog Card Number: 58-12902

PRINTED IN THE UNITED STATES OF AMERICA

The Little Farm

Farmer Small lives
on a farm.
He gets up early
in the morning.

He goes to the barn to feed the animals. They are all very hungry.

He milks the cows.

He strains the milk
into the milk cans.
He sets them in the
milk cooler.

Farmer Small takes the cows to pasture.

Farmer Small leaves
the cans of milk
on the milkstand.
The milk truck takes them
to the dairy.

Farmer Small feeds
the pigs.
They are
very hungry!

So are
    the chickens,
    the ducks
and
    the turkeys!

At noon,
Farmer Small goes
   to the mailbox
   and gets his mail.

Farmer Small
has a tractor
to help him
with his work.

In the spring,
Farmer Small plows
the field
with his tractor.

He harrows
the field
with his tractor.

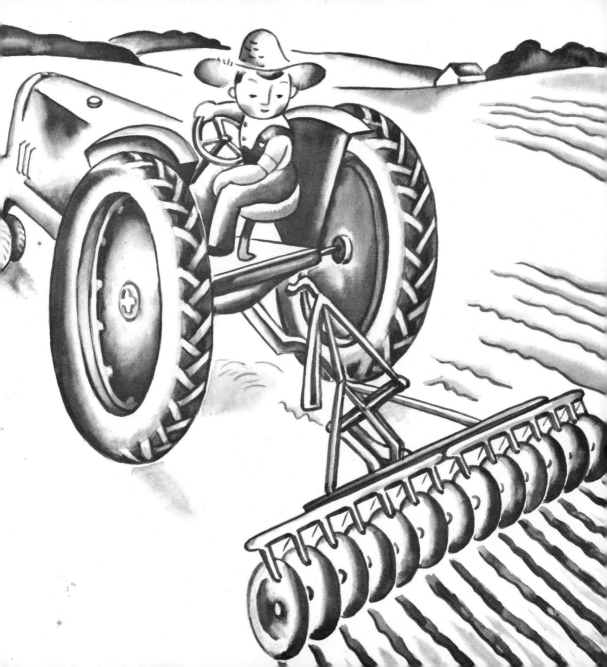

In the summer,
Farmer Small
cuts his hay
with his tractor.

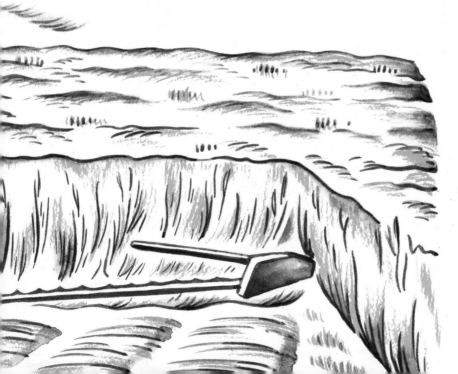

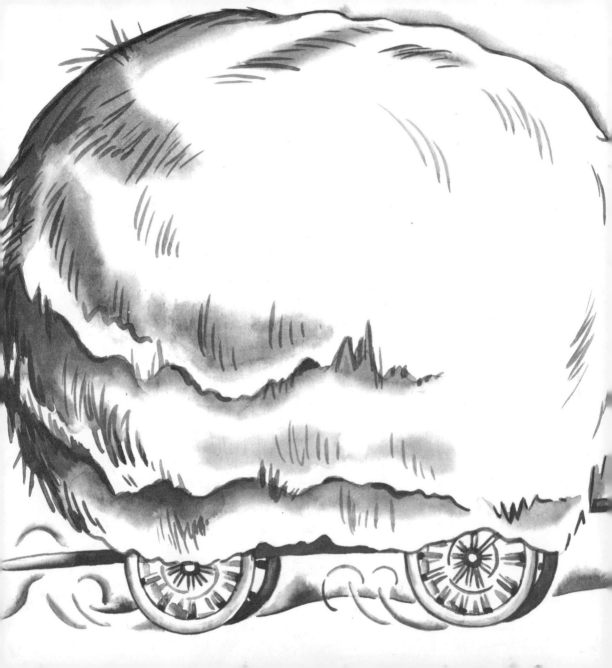

He hauls the loads of hay
to the barn.

In the fall,
Farmer Small
    picks apples
    in his orchard.

He hauls them
in the trailer
behind the tractor.

He sells them
at his
roadside stand.

In the winter,
Farmer Small
    chops his firewood.

He hauls the wood
on his bobsled
with his team.

Each day,
when evening comes,
Farmer Small gathers
the eggs.

He brings the cows
in from the pasture
and milks them.

Then
he goes into the house
to eat his supper—
and the sun goes down.

And
that's all—
about
Farmer Small!